Modern Digital Marketing: Strategies for a Connected World

AF484847

By Nacu Maria

MARIA NACU

Modern Digital Marketing: Strategies for a Connected World

Practical Insights and Tools for Effective Online Engagement

MODERN DIGITAL MARKETING STRATEGIES FOR A CONNECTED WORLD

Table of Contents

- 7.3 Actionable Next Steps for Readers

Chapter 1: Fundamentals of Digital Marketing

1.1 What is Digital Marketing?

Digital marketing is the promotion of products, services, or brands through electronic media, primarily the internet. It differs significantly from traditional marketing methods by enabling businesses to reach a broader audience through various digital channels, providing real-time data and measurable results.

Key Aspects of Digital Marketing:

- **Global Reach**: Allows businesses to connect with audiences worldwide.
- **Cost-Effective**: More budget-friendly compared to traditional advertising.
- **Interactive Engagement**: Enables direct interaction with consumers through social media, emails, and other digital platforms.
- **Data-Driven**: Facilitates analysis and tracking of campaigns to improve strategies.

The Importance of Digital Marketing:

In today's connected world, digital marketing is essential for businesses to remain competitive. It provides opportunities for brand visibility, customer engagement, and ultimately, growth. For individuals, understanding digital marketing is crucial for personal branding and career advancement.

1.2 Key Components of Digital Marketing

MODERN DIGITAL MARKETING STRATEGIES FOR A CONNECTED WORLD

Digital marketing encompasses various components, each crucial for an effective strategy:

1.2.1 Search Engine Optimization (SEO)

SEO involves optimizing your website and content to rank higher in search engine results. It includes:

- **On-Page SEO**: Optimizing individual web pages to rank higher and earn more relevant traffic. This involves content quality, keywords, meta tags, and internal linking.
- **Off-Page SEO**: Building external links and social signals to improve the site's authority and search engine ranking.
- **Technical SEO**: Enhancing the website's backend to improve its crawlability, speed, and performance.

Benefits: Increased visibility, organic traffic, and credibility.

1.2.2 Content Marketing

Content Marketing focuses on creating, publishing, and distributing valuable content to attract and retain a target audience.

- **Types of Content**: Blogs, videos, infographics, eBooks, podcasts.
- **Content Strategy**: Developing a plan to create and distribute content that aligns with business goals and audience needs.
- **SEO Integration**: Ensuring content is optimized for search engines to increase discoverability.

Benefits: Builds trust, educates consumers, and drives conversions.

1.2.3 Social Media Marketing

Social Media Marketing uses social platforms to promote products and engage with consumers.

- **Platforms**: Facebook, Instagram, Twitter, LinkedIn, TikTok.
- **Strategies**: Content creation, paid advertising, community engagement, influencer partnerships.
- **Metrics**: Likes, shares, comments, followers, engagement rate.

Benefits: Enhances brand awareness, fosters community, and drives traffic.

1.2.4 Email Marketing

Email Marketing involves sending targeted messages to a list of subscribers to promote products, share news, or build relationships.

- **Campaign Types**: Newsletters, promotional emails, transactional emails, re-engagement emails.
- **List Building**: Collecting email addresses through lead magnets, sign-up forms, or social media.
- **Automation**: Using tools to send personalized emails based on user behavior and preferences.

Benefits: Direct communication, high ROI, and personalization.

1.2.5 Paid Advertising

MODERN DIGITAL MARKETING STRATEGIES FOR A CONNECTED WORLD

Paid Advertising involves paying for ad placements on various platforms to drive traffic and conversions.

- **Types**: Pay-Per-Click (PPC), display ads, social media ads, native advertising.
- **Platforms**: Google Ads, Facebook Ads, LinkedIn Ads, Bing Ads.
- **Targeting**: Demographics, interests, behavior, retargeting.

Benefits: Immediate visibility, targeted reach, and measurable results.

1.3 Digital Marketing vs. Traditional Marketing

Digital Marketing and **Traditional Marketing** serve the same purpose but operate differently.

Differences:

- **Channels**: Digital uses online channels (social media, email), while traditional uses offline channels (print, TV, radio).
- **Measurability**: Digital marketing offers precise metrics and analytics, while traditional relies more on estimates.
- **Interactivity**: Digital allows for direct engagement with consumers; traditional is more one-way.

Synergies:

- Combining both can create a comprehensive strategy that leverages the strengths of each approach. For example, a traditional TV campaign can drive traffic to an online store, while digital ads can reinforce brand recognition established through traditional media.

1.4 Understanding the Digital Customer Journey

The digital customer journey encompasses the stages a consumer goes through from awareness to loyalty. It includes:

- **Awareness**: The consumer becomes aware of a need or problem.
- **Consideration**: The consumer evaluates options to solve the problem.
- **Decision**: The consumer chooses a solution and makes a purchase.
- **Loyalty**: Post-purchase behavior, including repeat purchases and brand advocacy.

Importance: Understanding this journey helps in tailoring marketing strategies to guide consumers smoothly through each stage, enhancing their experience and increasing conversion rates.

Chapter 2: Strategies and Techniques

2.1 SEO: Optimizing for Search Engines

Search Engine Optimization (SEO) is the practice of improving your website's visibility on search engines like Google, Bing, and Yahoo. It involves a mix of technical and creative elements to boost rankings, drive traffic, and increase awareness.

2.1.1 On-Page SEO

On-Page SEO focuses on optimizing individual web pages to rank higher and earn more relevant traffic.

1. **Keyword Research and Implementation**
   - **Identify Relevant Keywords**: Start by researching keywords that your target audience uses. Tools like Google Keyword Planner, SEMrush, and Ahrefs can help identify high-traffic keywords relevant to your content.
   - **Example**: A local coffee shop might target keywords such as "best coffee near me" or "how to brew espresso at home."
   - **Incorporate Keywords Naturally**: Integrate these keywords into your titles, headings, and body text in a natural and engaging manner.

2. **Content Optimization**
   - **High-Quality Content**: Write informative and engaging content that addresses your audience's needs. Each piece of content should provide value and be well-structured

with headings, subheadings, and bullet points.

- **Example**: A blog post titled "How to Brew the Perfect Espresso" could include detailed instructions, images, and a short video.
- **Meta Tags**: Optimize meta titles and descriptions with primary keywords. These tags summarize the content of your page and appear in search engine results.
- **Example**: Meta description for the espresso post: "Learn the secrets to brewing the perfect espresso at home with our step-by-step guide."

3. **Technical SEO**

   - **URL Structure**: Use clean, descriptive URLs that include keywords. Avoid long, complex URLs.
   - **Example**: A URL like www.coffeeshop.com/best-espresso-techniques is more effective than www.coffeeshop.com/page1.
   - **Page Speed**: Optimize images, enable browser caching, and minimize code to improve loading times.
   - **Mobile Optimization**: Ensure your website is responsive and performs well on mobile devices.

4. **Internal Linking**

   - **Link Related Content**: Connect relevant pages within your site to improve navigation and SEO. This helps users discover more content and keeps them engaged longer.

- ○ **Example**: A blog post on espresso could link to another article about "Different Types of Coffee Beans."

2.1.2 Off-Page SEO

Off-Page SEO focuses on improving your website's authority and trustworthiness through external activities.

1. **Backlink Building**
   - ○ **Acquire Quality Backlinks**: Earn links from reputable and relevant websites. Backlinks act as votes of confidence, signaling to search engines that your site is trustworthy.
   - ○ **Strategies**: Create high-quality, shareable content that naturally attracts links. Reach out to other sites for guest blogging opportunities.
   - ○ **Example**: A coffee shop might write a guest post on a popular food blog about "Emerging Coffee Trends" with a link back to their website.

2. **Social Signals**
   - ○ **Boost Engagement**: Active participation on social media can enhance your SEO by driving traffic and engagement to your content.
   - ○ **Example**: Sharing a popular blog post about coffee recipes on social media and encouraging followers to share their own

recipes.

3. **Local SEO**
   - **Optimize for Local Searches**: Ensure your business is listed on Google My Business and other local directories. Provide accurate and consistent information across all platforms.
   - **Example**: A coffee shop would list their address, hours, and contact information accurately and keep it updated.

2.1.3 Monitoring and Analysis

1. **Use Analytics Tools**
   - **Track Performance**: Use tools like Google Analytics and Google Search Console to monitor key metrics such as organic traffic, bounce rates, and keyword rankings.
   - **Example**: Analyze which blog posts drive the most traffic and refine your content strategy based on these insights.
2. **Adjust Strategies**
   - **Continuous Improvement**: SEO is an ongoing process. Regularly review your performance data and adjust your strategies to improve your rankings and user engagement.

2.2 Content Marketing: Creating Valuable Content

MODERN DIGITAL MARKETING STRATEGIES FOR A CONNECTED WORLD

Content marketing involves creating and sharing valuable content to attract and engage your audience. It builds trust, provides information, and can lead to conversions.

2.2.1 Content Strategy

1. **Define Your Goals**
   - **Awareness**: Increase brand visibility and reach.
   - **Engagement**: Foster a deeper connection with your audience.
   - **Conversions**: Drive leads and sales.
   - **Example**: A coffee shop may want to build an online community of coffee enthusiasts or attract more local customers.

2. **Understand Your Audience**
   - **Create Personas**: Develop detailed profiles of your ideal customers. These personas should include demographics, interests, and pain points.
   - **Example**: "John," a busy professional, may be interested in quick coffee brewing techniques, while "Sarah," a college student, might enjoy experimenting with new recipes.

3. **Develop a Content Calendar**
   - **Plan Your Content**: Schedule content types and publication dates to ensure a consistent flow of engaging material.
   - **Example**: Plan weekly blog posts on different brewing methods and daily Instagram updates

showcasing new drinks.

2.2.2 Types of Content

1. **Blogging**
   - **Write SEO-Friendly Posts**: Create blog posts that address relevant topics and integrate keywords naturally.
   - **Example**: "The Ultimate Guide to Cold Brew Coffee" might include steps, tips, and common mistakes to avoid.

2. **Video Content**
   - **Produce Engaging Videos**: Use video content to provide tutorials, product demos, or behind-the-scenes looks.
   - **Example**: A video titled "How to Make Latte Art" could demonstrate techniques and be shared on YouTube and social media.

3. **Infographics**
   - **Visual Data Presentation**: Infographics help present complex information clearly and engagingly.
   - **Example**: An infographic on "The Journey of Coffee from Bean to Cup" could be shared on social media to educate and attract viewers.

4. **Podcasts**
   - **Host Engaging Discussions**: Use podcasts to discuss industry trends, interview experts, or share stories.

- **Example**: A coffee shop could have a podcast episode discussing the cultural significance of coffee in different countries.

2.2.3 Content Distribution

1. **Owned Media**
   - **Website and Blog**: Publish content on your website and ensure it is optimized for search engines.
   - **Email Newsletters**: Regularly update your subscribers with new content and exclusive offers.
   - **Example**: Send a monthly newsletter featuring blog highlights and upcoming events.
2. **Earned Media**
   - **Encourage Sharing**: Promote your content on social media and encourage followers to share it.
   - **Example**: Offer a downloadable guide in exchange for social shares.
3. **Paid Media**
   - **Promote Content**: Use paid advertising to boost your content's reach on social media or other platforms.
   - **Example**: Run a Facebook Ad campaign promoting a popular blog post about coffee brewing.

2.2.4 Measurement and Optimization

1. **Analyze Performance**
   - **Use Analytics**: Track content performance using tools like Google Analytics to measure metrics such as page views, engagement rates, and conversions.
   - **Example**: Review which blog posts generate the most traffic and engagement to refine future content strategies.

2. **Refine Strategies**
   - **Continuous Improvement**: Use performance data to adjust your content approach, focusing on what resonates most with your audience.

2.3 Social Media Marketing

Social media marketing involves using platforms like Facebook, Instagram, Twitter, and LinkedIn to connect with your audience, build brand awareness, and drive traffic.

2.3.1 Platform Selection

1. **Choose the Right Platforms**
   - **Identify Audience Preferences**: Different platforms cater to different demographics and content types.
   - **Example**: Use Instagram for visual content and a younger audience, LinkedIn for B2B marketing and professional content.

2.3.2 Content Creation

1. **Create Engaging Content**
   - **Use Visuals and Interactive Elements**: High-quality images, videos, and interactive features like polls and quizzes can increase engagement.
   - **Example**: Post a high-resolution photo of a new seasonal drink with a caption inviting followers to try it and share their feedback.

2. **Leverage Stories and Live Videos**
   - **Engage in Real-Time**: Use Stories on Instagram or Facebook and live videos to share timely updates and promotions.
   - **Example**: Host an Instagram Live session to demonstrate a new brewing technique and answer viewer questions.

2.3.3 Community Management

1. **Build Relationships**
   - **Engage with Followers**: Respond to comments and messages to build a sense of community.
   - **Example**: Respond to customer comments about their favorite drinks and feature user-generated content on your profile.

2. **Encourage User-Generated Content**
   - **Promote Community Participation**: Encourage followers to share their own photos and experiences using branded

hashtags.

- ○ **Example:** Run a contest asking followers to share their best coffee moments using the hashtag #MyCoffeeMoment.

2.3.4 Analytics and Optimization

Analytics and optimization are crucial to refining your social media marketing strategy and ensuring its effectiveness. Regularly analyzing your social media performance helps you understand what works and what doesn't, enabling you to make data-driven decisions.

1. Setting Up Analytics

To get started with social media analytics, ensure you have access to the necessary tools and data:

- **Platform Analytics**: Most social media platforms offer built-in analytics tools. For example, Facebook Insights, Instagram Insights, Twitter Analytics, and LinkedIn Analytics provide comprehensive data on your performance.
- **Third-Party Tools**: Consider using tools like Hootsuite, Buffer, or Sprout Social for more advanced analytics and reporting capabilities.

Example: Use Facebook Insights to track metrics like page views, post reach, and engagement. Monitor Instagram Insights for follower demographics and post interactions.

2. Key Metrics to Track

Understanding which metrics are most relevant to your goals is essential for effective social media analytics.

- **Engagement Rate**: This metric measures the level of interaction with your content, including likes, comments, shares, and clicks. High engagement indicates that your content resonates with your audience.
- **Follower Growth**: Track the increase or decrease in followers over time. Rapid growth can signal successful campaigns, while a plateau might indicate a need for new strategies.
- **Reach and Impressions**: Reach refers to the number of unique users who see your content, while impressions indicate how many times your content is displayed. Monitoring these metrics helps gauge your content's visibility.
- **Click-Through Rate (CTR)**: This metric shows the percentage of users who click on a link within your post. It's a good indicator of how compelling your calls-to-action are.
- **Conversion Rate**: Measures how effectively your social media efforts drive users to take a desired action, such as making a purchase or signing up for a newsletter.

Example: If you run a campaign on Instagram to promote a new coffee blend, monitor the engagement rate on posts, the number of new followers gained, and the click-through rate on links to your online store.

3. Analyzing Performance

Regularly analyze your social media metrics to gain insights into your audience's behavior and preferences.

- **Identify Trends**: Look for patterns in engagement and reach over time. For example, you might find that posts with videos or certain types of images generate higher engagement.
- **Content Performance**: Determine which types of content perform best. Analyze posts that receive the most likes, shares, and comments to understand what resonates with your audience.
- **Audience Demographics**: Use demographic data to tailor your content to the preferences of your followers. Insights on age, gender, location, and interests can guide your content creation.

Example: Analyze the performance of different types of content (photos, videos, text posts) on your Facebook page to identify what your audience engages with most. Adjust your content strategy to focus on high-performing formats.

4. Optimizing Your Strategy

Based on your analysis, make data-driven adjustments to your social media strategy.

- **Refine Content**: Create more of the content types that drive the highest engagement and reach. Experiment with new formats and topics to keep your audience interested.
- **Adjust Posting Times**: Identify the times of day when your audience is most active and schedule your posts

accordingly to maximize visibility and interaction.

- **Test and Iterate**: Use A/B testing to compare different versions of posts, such as varying the call-to-action or using different images. Analyze the results to determine which approach works best.

Example: If analysis shows that posts with behind-the-scenes videos generate the most engagement on Instagram, focus on creating more video content and test different video lengths and styles to optimize engagement further.

5. Reporting and Continuous Improvement

Regularly report on your social media performance to stakeholders and use insights for continuous improvement.

- **Create Reports**: Generate regular reports that summarize key metrics, trends, and insights. Use these reports to communicate your social media performance to your team or clients.
- **Set New Goals**: Based on your performance data, set new objectives for your social media strategy. Aim to improve key metrics like engagement rates, follower growth, and conversion rates over time.

Example: Create a monthly report that includes metrics such as engagement rate, follower growth, and top-performing posts. Use the insights from these reports to set new goals, such as increasing the engagement rate by 10% in the next quarter.

By consistently monitoring and optimizing your social media efforts, you can enhance your online presence, better connect with your audience, and achieve your marketing objectives more effectively.

2.4 Email Marketing

Email marketing is a direct and highly effective way to communicate with your audience, build relationships, and drive sales. It allows you to send personalized messages and offers straight to your customers' inboxes.

2.4.1 Building Your Email List

Building a robust email list is the first step in a successful email marketing strategy.

- **Offer Incentives**: Encourage people to subscribe by offering valuable incentives, such as discounts, exclusive content, or free resources. For instance, a coffee shop might offer a free eBook on coffee brewing techniques in exchange for email sign-ups.
- **Sign-Up Forms**: Place sign-up forms prominently on your website, blog, and social media profiles. Use pop-ups and slide-ins to capture more leads without being intrusive.

Example: A coffee shop could use a pop-up on their website offering a 10% discount on the first order for newsletter subscribers.

2.4.2 Crafting Effective Emails

Creating engaging and effective emails involves several key elements:

- **Compelling Subject Lines**: Write attention-grabbing subject lines to increase open rates. For example,

"Discover Our Secret Recipe for the Perfect Espresso" could entice subscribers to open the email.

- **Engaging Content**: Ensure that your emails provide value to the reader. This might include informative articles, promotional offers, or exclusive updates.
- **Clear Calls-to-Action (CTAs)**: Include clear and compelling CTAs that guide recipients on what to do next, such as visiting your website or redeeming a discount code.

Example: An email promoting a new coffee blend could include a subject line like "New Flavor Alert: Try Our Limited Edition Espresso" and a CTA button saying "Shop Now."

2.4.3 Segmenting Your Audience

Segmenting your email list allows you to send more targeted and relevant messages.

- **Demographic Segmentation**: Group subscribers by demographics such as age, gender, and location.
- **Behavioral Segmentation**: Segment based on past interactions, such as purchase history or engagement with previous emails.

Example: A coffee shop might create a segment for customers who frequently purchase specialty blends and send them targeted offers on new arrivals.

2.4.4 Automation and Personalization

Automation and personalization enhance the effectiveness of your email marketing efforts.

- **Automated Workflows**: Set up automated workflows for different scenarios, such as welcoming new subscribers, following up on abandoned carts, or sending birthday offers.
- **Personalized Content**: Use subscriber data to personalize email content. Address recipients by their first name and tailor recommendations based on their preferences.

Example: A welcome email series could start with a thank you message, followed by an introduction to the coffee shop's story, and end with a special discount offer.

2.4.5 Measuring Success

Track the performance of your email campaigns to understand their impact and improve future efforts.

- **Open Rates**: Measure the percentage of recipients who open your emails.
- **Click-Through Rates (CTR)**: Track how many recipients click on links within your emails.
- **Conversion Rates**: Measure the number of recipients who complete a desired action, such as making a purchase or signing up for an event.

Example: If an email campaign promoting a new product has a high open rate but a low click-through rate, you might need to improve the email's content or CTAs.

2.4.6 Continuous Optimization

Based on your performance data, continuously refine your email marketing strategy.

- **A/B Testing**: Test different elements of your emails, such as subject lines, images, or CTAs, to see what performs best.
- **Feedback and Surveys**: Use feedback and surveys to gather insights from your subscribers about what they find valuable.

Example: Test two different subject lines for a promotional email to determine which one leads to higher open rates. Use the winning subject line format for future campaigns.

By effectively managing your email list, crafting engaging emails, and continuously optimizing your approach, you can maximize the impact of your email marketing efforts.

Conclusion of Chapter 2

By implementing these strategies and techniques, you can enhance your digital marketing efforts and better connect with your audience. Whether through SEO, content marketing, social media, or email marketing, each approach offers unique benefits and can be tailored to fit your specific needs and objectives in the digital landscape. Continuous monitoring and optimization are key to maintaining and improving your digital marketing performance over time.

Chapter 3: Tools and Resources

In this chapter, we'll explore various tools and resources that can enhance your digital marketing efforts. These tools help streamline processes, improve efficiency, and provide valuable insights to guide your strategy. From analytics platforms to content management systems, we'll cover essential tools for different aspects of digital marketing.

3.1 Analytics and Reporting

Understanding your audience and measuring the performance of your marketing activities is crucial for making informed decisions. Analytics and reporting tools provide insights into traffic, engagement, conversions, and more.

3.1.1 Google Analytics

Google Analytics is a powerful tool for tracking website performance.

- **Setup**: Start by setting up Google Analytics for your website. Add the tracking code to your site to begin collecting data.
- **Key Metrics**: Monitor metrics such as sessions, bounce rate, page views, and average session duration. These metrics give you an overview of how visitors interact with your site.
- **Behavior Flow**: Analyze the Behavior Flow report to understand the path users take through your site. This helps identify popular pages and potential drop-off points.
- **Goals and Conversions**: Set up goals to track specific

actions, such as form submissions or product purchases. This provides insights into how well your site converts visitors into leads or customers.

Example: A coffee shop can use Google Analytics to track how many visitors read their blog on coffee brewing techniques and how many proceed to purchase coffee beans from their online store.

3.1.2 Social Media Analytics

Each social media platform offers built-in analytics tools that provide insights into your social media performance.

- **Facebook Insights**: Track metrics such as page likes, post reach, and engagement. Use this data to understand what types of content resonate most with your audience.
- **Instagram Insights**: Analyze follower demographics, engagement, and reach. Monitor the performance of posts, Stories, and IGTV videos.
- **Twitter Analytics**: View metrics like tweet impressions, profile visits, and follower growth. Use these insights to refine your Twitter strategy.
- **LinkedIn Analytics**: Monitor page views, engagement, and follower demographics. Analyze the performance of posts and updates.

Example: By analyzing Instagram Insights, a coffee shop might find that posts with behind-the-scenes videos generate higher engagement than static images, leading them to focus more on video content.

3.1.3 Email Marketing Analytics

Email marketing platforms provide detailed analytics on your campaigns.

- **Open Rates**: Track the percentage of recipients who open your emails. High open rates indicate compelling subject lines.
- **Click-Through Rates (CTR)**: Measure how many recipients click on links within your emails. This metric reflects the effectiveness of your email content and CTAs.
- **Conversion Rates**: Monitor how many recipients complete a desired action, such as making a purchase or signing up for an event.

Example: A coffee shop running an email campaign to promote a new coffee blend can use email analytics to track how many subscribers open the email, click on the product link, and make a purchase.

3.2 Automation Tools

Automation tools help streamline repetitive tasks, allowing you to focus on strategic activities.

3.2.1 Email Automation

Automate your email marketing campaigns to improve efficiency and personalization.

- **Welcome Series**: Set up automated welcome emails for new subscribers. These emails can introduce your brand and offer initial value, such as a discount code or a useful guide.

- **Drip Campaigns**: Create drip campaigns that send a series of emails over time. This keeps your audience engaged with relevant content based on their interactions.
- **Behavioral Triggers**: Use behavioral triggers to send emails based on user actions, such as abandoning a cart or visiting a specific page on your website.

Example: A coffee shop might automate a welcome series that includes a thank you email, an introduction to their products, and a discount code for the first purchase.

3.2.2 Social Media Scheduling

Automate your social media posting to maintain a consistent presence without the need to manually post every day.

- **Scheduling Tools**: Use tools like Hootsuite, Buffer, or Sprout Social to schedule posts across multiple platforms in advance.
- **Content Calendar**: Plan your social media content with a calendar to ensure you cover all important events and promotions.

Example: A coffee shop can schedule posts about daily specials, upcoming events, and seasonal promotions to ensure they are shared consistently without manual effort each day.

3.3 SEO Tools

SEO tools help you optimize your website and content to improve search engine rankings.

3.3.1 Keyword Research Tools

Identify the best keywords to target for your SEO efforts.

- **Google Keyword Planner**: Provides keyword ideas and search volume data.
- **Ahrefs**: Offers comprehensive keyword research, competitor analysis, and backlink tracking.
- **SEMrush**: Combines keyword research with competitive analysis and site auditing features.

Example: A coffee shop can use Ahrefs to discover high-traffic keywords related to coffee brewing and incorporate them into their blog posts.

3.3.2 On-Page SEO Tools

Optimize your website content for better search engine performance.

- **Yoast SEO**: A WordPress plugin that helps optimize content with real-time feedback on readability, keyword usage, and meta tags.
- **Screaming Frog**: An SEO spider tool that analyzes your site's structure, identifies technical issues, and suggests improvements.

Example: Using Yoast SEO, a coffee shop can ensure their blog posts are optimized for readability and keyword integration.

3.3.3 Backlink Analysis Tools

Monitor and analyze your backlink profile.

- **Moz Link Explorer**: Provides insights into your backlink profile and identifies opportunities for link building.

- **Majestic**: Offers detailed analysis of backlinks, including trust flow and citation flow metrics.

Example: A coffee shop can use Moz Link Explorer to analyze their backlinks and identify opportunities for acquiring more high-quality links.

3.4 Content Management Systems (CMS)

A Content Management System (CMS) is essential for creating, managing, and optimizing your digital content.

3.4.1 WordPress

WordPress is a popular CMS known for its flexibility and ease of use.

- **Customization**: Choose from thousands of themes and plugins to customize your website's appearance and functionality.
- **SEO-Friendly**: Use plugins like Yoast SEO to optimize your content and improve your search engine rankings.

Example: A coffee shop can use WordPress to build a blog that shares coffee recipes, brewing tips, and product updates.

3.4.2 HubSpot CMS

HubSpot CMS offers a powerful platform for managing content and integrating with marketing tools.

- **All-In-One Solution**: Combines CMS functionality with marketing automation, CRM, and analytics.
- **Personalization**: Use HubSpot's tools to personalize content based on user behavior and preferences.

Example: A coffee shop using HubSpot CMS can create targeted landing pages for different customer segments and track their interactions through the CRM.

3.4.3 Shopify

Shopify is ideal for businesses focused on eCommerce.

- **eCommerce Features**: Offers tools for product management, payment processing, and shipping integration.
- **SEO and Marketing**: Includes built-in SEO features and integrates with various marketing tools.

Example: A coffee shop selling beans and brewing equipment online can use Shopify to manage their inventory, process orders, and optimize their online store for search engines.

3.5 Design and Multimedia Tools

Design and multimedia tools help create visually appealing content that engages your audience.

3.5.1 Graphic Design Tools

Create graphics for your website, social media, and marketing materials.

- **Canva**: A user-friendly design tool that offers templates for social media posts, flyers, infographics, and more.
- **Adobe Photoshop**: A professional tool for creating and editing images with advanced features.

Example: A coffee shop can use Canva to design promotional graphics for new products or events.

3.5.2 Video Editing Tools

Produce and edit high-quality video content.

- **Adobe Premiere Pro**: A professional video editing software with comprehensive features for creating polished videos.
- **iMovie**: A user-friendly option for Mac users to edit videos quickly and easily.

Example: A coffee shop might use Adobe Premiere Pro to edit a video tutorial on latte art, adding music, text overlays, and transitions.

3.5.3 Audio Tools

Enhance your audio content, including podcasts and background music for videos.

- **Audacity**: A free, open-source tool for recording and editing audio.
- **Adobe Audition**: A professional tool for advanced audio editing and production.

Example: A coffee shop could use Audacity to edit a podcast episode about the origins of their coffee beans, improving sound quality and adding effects.

Conclusion of Chapter 3

By utilizing these tools and resources, you can streamline your digital marketing efforts, enhance your content, and gain valuable insights into your audience's behavior. Whether it's analytics, automation, SEO, content management, or design, each tool offers unique benefits that can be tailored to fit your specific needs and objectives in the dynamic field of digital marketing.

Chapter 4: Case Studies

In this chapter, we explore the practical applications of digital marketing strategies through real-world case studies. These examples highlight both successful campaigns and notable failures, providing valuable insights into effective techniques and common pitfalls. By analyzing these cases, you can better understand how to apply digital marketing principles in your own efforts and avoid mistakes that could hinder your success.

4.1 Successful Digital Campaigns

Studying successful digital marketing campaigns helps illuminate effective strategies and innovative approaches. Here, we delve into three notable campaigns that achieved remarkable success.

4.1.1 Old Spice: "The Man Your Man Could Smell Like"

The Old Spice campaign "The Man Your Man Could Smell Like," launched in 2010, is a textbook example of how a creative approach can breathe new life into a traditional brand.

Campaign Overview: The campaign featured a series of humorous commercials starring Isaiah Mustafa, aiming to reposition Old Spice as a modern, appealing brand for younger audiences while retaining its long-standing reputation. The campaign used a mix of traditional and digital media, focusing heavily on YouTube and social media platforms.

Execution:

- **Content Creation**: The commercials combined humor, absurd scenarios, and a charismatic spokesperson to capture attention. Mustafa's character directly addressed the audience, creating a memorable and engaging viewing experience.

- **Multichannel Distribution**: Initially aired on television, the commercials were quickly uploaded to YouTube, where they went viral. Old Spice also leveraged social media platforms to interact with fans, creating personalized video responses to user comments and tweets.

Impact:

- **Viral Success**: The campaign's videos garnered millions of views on YouTube within days of their release. The humorous and shareable nature of the content led to widespread online sharing.
- **Sales Surge**: Following the campaign's launch, Old Spice saw a 125% increase in body wash sales, and the brand's market share in the body wash category significantly improved◇27†source◇ .

Lessons Learned:

- **Creativity and Humor**: Leveraging humor and creativity can make a campaign more engaging and shareable.
- **Direct Engagement**: Interacting with fans and creating personalized content can deepen engagement and foster brand loyalty.
- **Cross-Platform Strategy**: Utilizing both traditional and digital channels can amplify reach and

effectiveness.

4.1.2 Nike: "Breaking2"

Nike's "Breaking2" campaign showcases how creating a compelling narrative around a significant challenge can captivate audiences and enhance brand perception.

Campaign Overview: In 2017, Nike embarked on an ambitious project to break the two-hour marathon barrier. The "Breaking2" campaign was designed to document and promote this attempt, emphasizing innovation and athletic achievement.

Execution:

- **Live Event**: Nike organized a live marathon event, where elite runners attempted to complete the marathon in under two hours. The event was livestreamed on Twitter and Facebook, attracting millions of viewers globally.
- **Content Marketing**: Leading up to the event, Nike produced a series of documentaries and articles detailing the preparation, technology, and science involved in the attempt. This content was distributed through Nike's website and social media channels.
- **Engagement**: Nike used social media to provide real-time updates, interactive content, and behind-the-scenes looks at the training and technology involved.

Impact:

- **Global Engagement**: The livestream attracted over 13 million views, creating a significant buzz around the event. The campaign generated widespread media coverage and discussions on social media.

- **Brand Positioning**: Nike reinforced its image as a pioneer in sports innovation and a supporter of athletes striving for groundbreaking achievements .

Lessons Learned:

- **Compelling Storytelling**: Building a narrative around a bold challenge or goal can capture the imagination of your audience.
- **Real-Time Interaction**: Livestreaming events and providing real-time updates create a sense of immediacy and involvement.
- **Integrated Content Strategy**: Combining live events with supporting content and social media engagement can enhance the overall impact of a campaign.

4.1.3 Dove: "Real Beauty Sketches"

Dove's "Real Beauty Sketches" campaign is an exemplary case of how addressing social issues can resonate deeply with audiences and enhance brand perception.

Campaign Overview: Launched in 2013, Dove's campaign featured a forensic artist sketching women based on their own descriptions and then based on others' descriptions. The resulting sketches highlighted the disparity between self-perception and how others see them, promoting a message of real beauty.

Execution:

- **Central Video**: The campaign's central video was posted on YouTube and quickly went viral due to its emotional and thought-provoking content.
- **Social Media**: Dove encouraged viewers to share the video and discuss their reactions on social media. The campaign also involved partnerships with influencers and media outlets to broaden its reach.
- **Earned Media**: The campaign garnered extensive media coverage, with numerous articles and discussions about its impact on perceptions of beauty.

Impact:

- **High Engagement**: The video received over 114 million views in its first month, making it one of the most-watched video ads at the time.
- **Positive Brand Image**: The campaign significantly improved Dove's brand image by aligning with values of self-acceptance and real beauty .

Lessons Learned:

- **Emotional Resonance**: Campaigns that address personal and social issues can create strong emotional connections with audiences.
- **Viral Potential**: Creating content that resonates on a personal level can achieve widespread organic reach.
- **Strategic Partnerships**: Collaborating with

influencers and media can amplify the message and increase campaign visibility.

4.2 Lessons Learned from Failures

Analyzing failed campaigns can provide crucial insights into what to avoid in your digital marketing efforts. Here, we examine three campaigns that faced significant challenges and the lessons learned from their shortcomings.

4.2.1 Pepsi: "Live for Now"

Pepsi's "Live for Now" campaign faced a severe backlash due to its insensitivity towards social issues, resulting in a public relations crisis.

Campaign Overview: In 2017, Pepsi released an ad featuring Kendall Jenner participating in a protest and offering a can of Pepsi to a police officer, seemingly diffusing tension. The ad was intended to convey a message of unity and peace.

Execution:

- **Multimedia Launch**: The ad was promoted across television and digital platforms, including extensive social media coverage.
- **Celebrity Endorsement**: The use of Kendall Jenner aimed to attract a younger audience and leverage her social media influence.

Problems:

- **Insensitive Content**: The ad was criticized for trivializing serious social movements and issues of police brutality and racial equality.

- **Lack of Authenticity**: Viewers perceived the use of a celebrity in this context as inauthentic and opportunistic.

Impact:

- **Negative Backlash**: The ad sparked widespread outrage on social media and in the press, leading to the ad being pulled just days after its release. Pepsi issued a public apology in response to the backlash .

Lessons Learned:

- **Cultural Sensitivity**: Ensure that your content is sensitive to social and cultural contexts, avoiding the trivialization of serious issues.
- **Authenticity**: Avoid leveraging social issues or movements for commercial gain in a way that can be perceived as exploitative.
- **Crisis Management**: Be prepared to respond quickly and transparently to negative feedback and public relations crises.

4.2.2 McDonald's: "Dead Dad" Ad

McDonald's UK faced significant criticism for an ad that was perceived as exploiting emotional triggers inappropriately.

Campaign Overview: The 2017 UK ad depicted a boy struggling to connect with his deceased father, only to find a connection through their shared love for Filet-O-Fish sandwiches at McDonald's.

Execution:

- **Television and Online:** The ad was broadcast on television and shared online, intended to evoke emotional connections and nostalgia.

Problems:

- **Emotional Exploitation:** The ad was seen as manipulating grief for commercial purposes, using a sensitive subject to promote a product.
- **Consumer Backlash:** Both the public and advocacy groups criticized the ad for being in poor taste and insensitive.

Impact:

- **Ad Withdrawal:** Facing negative reactions, McDonald's withdrew the ad and issued a public apology .

Lessons Learned:

- **Appropriate Tone:** Handle sensitive topics with care and ensure the tone is respectful and appropriate.
- **Audience Testing:** Conduct thorough testing and seek feedback from focus groups to gauge potential reactions before launching a campaign.
- **Respect for Emotions:** Use emotional triggers judiciously and with respect for the audience's feelings, avoiding manipulation.

4.2.3 Coca-Cola: "New Coke"

Coca-Cola's introduction of "New Coke" in 1985 is a classic example of misjudging consumer loyalty and preferences.

Campaign Overview: In an attempt to compete with Pepsi, Coca-Cola introduced a new formula to replace its original Coke. The company believed the sweeter taste of New Coke would appeal to younger consumers and increase market share.

Execution:

- **Product Launch**: Coca-Cola launched New Coke with a significant marketing push, including television and print ads, and phased out the original formula.

Problems:

- **Consumer Attachment**: Coca-Cola underestimated the deep emotional attachment and brand loyalty consumers had to the original formula.
- **Negative Feedback**: Loyal customers reacted negatively, feeling betrayed by the change and demanding the return of the original Coke.

Impact:

- **Reintroduction**: Coca4.2.3 Coca-Cola: "New Coke" (continued)

4.2.3 Coca-Cola: "New Coke"

Coca-Cola's introduction of "New Coke" in 1985 stands as a notable example of how misreading consumer preferences can lead to significant backlash and a critical misstep in marketing strategy.

Campaign Overview: To compete with Pepsi's growing popularity, Coca-Cola introduced a new formula for its flagship product, intending to offer a sweeter taste that would appeal more to the younger generation and Pepsi drinkers. The company decided to replace the original Coke with the new version entirely, without retaining the classic formula.

Execution:

- **Market Launch**: Coca-Cola launched New Coke with extensive marketing efforts, including television commercials, print ads, and promotional events. The company expected the new formula to revitalize the brand and capture market share from Pepsi.
- **Elimination of Original Formula**: Coca-Cola phased out the original formula, positioning New Coke as the replacement. This decision was based on taste tests and market research that indicated a preference for the sweeter flavor.

Problems:

- **Consumer Loyalty Misjudgment**: Coca-Cola underestimated the strong emotional and nostalgic attachment consumers had to the original formula. Despite the market research, loyal customers felt betrayed by the discontinuation of a product that had become a part of their daily lives.
- **Negative Feedback**: The introduction of New Coke

led to a significant backlash from consumers who preferred the original taste. Protests, negative media coverage, and consumer complaints quickly mounted, showing that taste tests and research had failed to capture the depth of brand loyalty.

Impact:

- **Reintroduction of Original Formula**: Within just a few months of New Coke's launch, Coca-Cola reintroduced the original formula as "Coca-Cola Classic." The rapid consumer outcry forced the company to acknowledge its mistake and revert to the classic recipe.
- **Market Consequences**: The New Coke fiasco initially damaged Coca-Cola's brand image but ultimately reinforced consumer loyalty when the company listened to its customers and brought back the original formula .

Lessons Learned:

- **Understand Consumer Loyalty**: Deep emotional connections to a brand can outweigh market research and product development. Companies must recognize and respect the sentimental value that long-standing products hold for consumers.
- **Thorough Market Testing**: Extensive testing and phased rollouts can help identify potential issues before a full-scale product launch. Engage with core

consumers to understand their attachment to the existing product.

- **Flexibility and Adaptability**: Be prepared to respond quickly to negative feedback and adapt strategies accordingly. Coca-Cola's willingness to reintroduce the original formula demonstrated their commitment to customer satisfaction and helped recover brand trust.

Conclusion of Chapter 4

Chapter 4 highlighted the importance of learning from both successful and failed digital marketing campaigns. By examining real-world examples, we gleaned valuable insights into what drives success and how to avoid common pitfalls.

Successful Campaigns: The case studies of Old Spice, Nike, and Dove illustrate how creative content, compelling storytelling, and addressing social issues can lead to high engagement and positive brand perception. These campaigns successfully utilized digital platforms, engaged directly with audiences, and aligned their messages with the brand's core values and goals. They demonstrated the power of humor, innovation, and emotional resonance in creating impactful marketing efforts.

Failed Campaigns: On the other hand, the case studies of Pepsi, McDonald's, and Coca-Cola show the risks of misjudging audience sentiments and exploiting sensitive topics. These failures emphasize the need for cultural sensitivity, authenticity, and thorough market testing. Missteps in these areas can lead to significant backlash, damaging brand reputation and customer trust. However, they also highlight the importance of quick, transparent responses to consumer feedback and the ability to adapt strategies swiftly.

Chapter 5: Implementing Digital Marketing

In this chapter, we explore how to implement a digital marketing strategy effectively. From setting goals and budgeting to executing and monitoring campaigns, this chapter provides a comprehensive guide to bringing your digital marketing plans to fruition.

5.1 Creating a Digital Marketing Plan

A well-crafted digital marketing plan serves as a roadmap for your marketing efforts, outlining how you will achieve your goals and measure success. Here's a step-by-step approach to creating a robust digital marketing plan.

5.1.1 Setting Goals

Setting clear, actionable goals is the foundation of any successful digital marketing strategy. Goals provide direction and a way to measure your progress.

- **Define Objectives**: Start by identifying what you want to achieve. Objectives should be aligned with your overall business goals and can include increasing brand awareness, driving website traffic, generating leads, or boosting sales.
    - **SMART Goals**: Ensure your objectives are Specific, Measurable, Achievable, Relevant, and Time-bound. This framework helps in setting clear and realistic goals.
    - **Example**: Instead of a vague goal like "increase website traffic," set a SMART goal such as "increase website traffic by 25% within the next six months through

improved SEO and content marketing."

- **Prioritize Goals**: Determine which goals are most important to your business's success and focus on them. Balancing multiple goals can be challenging, so prioritize based on potential impact and feasibility.
  - Example: If generating leads is more critical than increasing social media followers, allocate more resources to lead generation activities.
- **Align with KPIs**: Identify Key Performance Indicators (KPIs) that will help measure the success of your goals. KPIs provide quantifiable measurements for your objectives.
  - Example: For a goal to increase website traffic, relevant KPIs might include the number of unique visitors, session duration, and bounce rate.

Sources:

- HubSpot on Setting SMART Goals[1]
- Neil Patel on Digital Marketing Goals

5.1.2 Budgeting

Effective budgeting ensures that you allocate resources efficiently to achieve your digital marketing goals.

- **Determine Total Budget**: Start by determining the total budget you can allocate to digital marketing. Consider your overall business finances and how much you can realistically spend.

---

1. https://blog.hubspot.com/marketing/smart-goals

- ○ **Example**: A small business might allocate 10-15% of their revenue to marketing efforts, adjusting based on specific needs and growth targets.
- **Break Down by Channels**: Divide your budget among various digital channels based on their expected ROI and alignment with your goals. Allocate funds to SEO, PPC advertising, social media, content creation, and email marketing.
  - ○ **Example**: Allocate 40% to PPC campaigns if they have previously driven significant traffic, 30% to content creation, 20% to social media, and 10% to SEO.
- **Include Tools and Resources**: Account for the cost of tools and resources required for your campaigns, such as marketing software, analytics tools, and external services like graphic design or copywriting.
  - ○ **Example**: Budget for a subscription to a social media management tool or an email marketing platform.
- **Plan for Contingencies**: Set aside a portion of your budget for unexpected expenses or opportunities. This ensures flexibility and the ability to adapt to changes or new trends.
  - ○ **Example**: Reserve 5-10% of your budget for contingency funds to handle unforeseen costs or capitalize on emergent trends.

Sources:

- CMI on Marketing Budget Allocation
- HubSpot on Marketing Budget[2]

---

2. https://blog.hubspot.com/marketing/marketing-budgets

5.2 Executing and Monitoring Campaigns

Execution and monitoring are critical phases in bringing your digital marketing plan to life. This involves launching your campaigns, tracking their performance, and making necessary adjustments.

5.2.1 Executing Campaigns

Once your plan is in place and your budget is allocated, it's time to execute your digital marketing campaigns.

- **Develop a Content Calendar**: Plan your content in advance using a content calendar. This helps in maintaining consistency and organizing your content marketing efforts.
  - Example: Create a monthly content calendar that includes blog posts, social media updates, email newsletters, and promotional campaigns.
- **Launch and Promote**: Execute your campaigns across the selected digital channels. Ensure that all promotional materials align with your brand messaging and objectives.
  - Example: Launch a social media ad campaign to coincide with a new product release, ensuring the messaging is consistent across Facebook, Instagram, and Twitter.
- **Utilize Automation**: Leverage automation tools to streamline campaign management. Automate email sequences, social media posts, and lead nurturing

processes to save time and ensure timely interactions.

- ○ **Example**: Use a tool like HubSpot to automate follow-up emails for new leads, based on their interactions with your website.

Sources:

- CoSchedule on Content Calendar
- HubSpot on Campaign Execution[3]

5.2.2 Monitoring Campaigns

Effective monitoring allows you to assess the performance of your campaigns and make data-driven decisions to optimize results.

- **Track Metrics and KPIs**: Regularly monitor the KPIs you identified in your planning phase. Use analytics tools to track metrics such as traffic, engagement, conversions, and ROI.
  - ○ **Example**: Use Google Analytics to track website traffic and conversion rates, and social media analytics tools to monitor engagement and follower growth.
- **Analyze Performance**: Evaluate the data collected to understand what's working and what's not. Look for patterns and trends that can inform your strategy.
  - ○ **Example**: Analyze which blog posts generate the most traffic and leads, and adjust your content strategy accordingly to focus on high-performing topics.
- **Adjust Strategies**: Based on your analysis, make

---

3. https://blog.hubspot.com/marketing/marketing-campaign-ideas

necessary adjustments to your campaigns. This might include reallocating budget, modifying content, or changing your targeting approach.

- ○ **Example**: If a particular ad set on Facebook is underperforming, experiment with new ad copy or targeting parameters to improve results.

- **Reporting**: Create regular reports to summarize campaign performance. Share these reports with stakeholders and use them to guide future strategy decisions.

  - ○ **Example**: Develop a monthly report that highlights key metrics, insights, and recommendations for upcoming campaigns.

Sources:

- Google Analytics Guide
- HubSpot on Monitoring Campaigns[4]

Conclusion of Chapter 5

Chapter 5 provided a comprehensive guide to implementing digital marketing strategies effectively.

Creating a Digital Marketing Plan: We discussed the importance of setting SMART goals, budgeting wisely, and understanding your target audience. A well-structured plan aligns your digital marketing efforts with your business objectives and ensures that resources are allocated effectively.

Executing and Monitoring Campaigns: Execution involves developing a content calendar, launching campaigns,

---

4. https://blog.hubspot.com/marketing/campaign-tracking

and utilizing automation tools to streamline processes. Monitoring and adjusting campaigns based on performance data is crucial for optimizing results and achieving your marketing goals.

Chapter 6: Trends and Future Directions

In this chapter, we explore the emerging technologies shaping the future of digital marketing and the evolving landscape of customer engagement. By understanding these trends, businesses can stay ahead of the curve and adapt their strategies to meet the changing expectations and behaviors of their audiences.

6.1 Emerging Technologies in Digital Marketing

The rapid advancement of technology is driving significant changes in how marketers interact with consumers. Here, we examine key technologies—Artificial Intelligence (AI), Voice Search, and Augmented/Virtual Reality (AR/VR)—that are transforming digital marketing.

6.1.1 Artificial Intelligence (AI)

Artificial Intelligence (AI) is becoming integral to digital marketing, offering new ways to analyze data, interact with customers, and create personalized experiences.

Applications of AI:

- **Data Analysis**: AI excels at analyzing large datasets to uncover patterns and insights that inform marketing strategies. Machine learning algorithms can predict customer behaviors and preferences, enabling more targeted marketing efforts.
    - **Example**: A retail brand uses AI to analyze purchase history and browsing data to recommend products to individual customers, increasing the likelihood of conversion.

- **Chatbots and Customer Support**: AI-powered chatbots provide real-time customer support, answering queries, and resolving issues efficiently. They can handle multiple interactions simultaneously, enhancing customer service capabilities.
  - Example: A bank uses an AI chatbot on its website to assist customers with account queries, balance checks, and transaction history, reducing the load on human support staff.
- **Personalized Marketing**: AI enables hyper-personalization, where marketing messages and content are tailored to the specific needs and preferences of each user. This can include personalized email campaigns, product recommendations, and dynamic content on websites.
  - Example: Spotify uses AI to create personalized playlists for users based on their listening habits, which enhances user engagement and retention.
- **Content Generation**: AI tools can assist in content creation by generating articles, social media posts, and even video scripts based on provided keywords and guidelines.
  - Example: A content marketing team uses AI to generate blog post outlines and draft social media updates, speeding up the content production process.

Impact and Future Directions:

- **Enhanced Personalization**: AI will continue to drive deeper personalization, making marketing more relevant and effective for individual consumers.

- **Automation of Tasks**: Routine marketing tasks will become increasingly automated, freeing marketers to focus on strategic and creative aspects.
- **Ethical Considerations**: As AI usage grows, issues related to data privacy, algorithmic transparency, and ethical AI deployment will become more prominent.

Sources:

- Forbes on AI in Marketing
- HubSpot on AI in Marketing[1]

6.1.2 Voice Search

Voice search is transforming how consumers find information and interact with technology, driven by the widespread adoption of voice-activated assistants.

Key Aspects of Voice Search:

- **Conversational Queries**: Voice searches are typically longer and more conversational than text-based queries, requiring marketers to optimize content for natural language and question-based searches.
  - **Example**: Instead of optimizing for "cheap flights," consider optimizing for "Where can I find cheap flights to New York?"
- **Featured Snippets and Quick Answers**: Voice assistants often provide answers from featured snippets, making it crucial for content to be structured

---

1. https://blog.hubspot.com/marketing/artificial-intelligence-marketing

to appear in these snippets.

- ○ **Example**: Creating a FAQ section on your website can increase the chances of your content being used as a source for voice search answers.
- **Local SEO**: Voice search is frequently used for local inquiries. Optimizing for local SEO, such as including location-specific keywords and ensuring business listings are accurate, can enhance visibility.
  - ○ **Example**: A local restaurant optimizes their Google My Business listing and uses local keywords like "best pizza in downtown" to attract voice search traffic.

Impact and Future Directions:

- **Changes in SEO Strategy**: Marketers will need to adapt their SEO strategies to focus more on natural language and conversational keywords.
- **Increased Adoption**: As more devices incorporate voice-activated technology, optimizing for voice search will become essential for maintaining search visibility.
- **Integration with Smart Devices**: Voice search will become more integrated with smart home devices, expanding its use cases beyond traditional search queries.

Sources:

- Moz on Voice Search Optimization
- Search Engine Journal on Voice Search

6.1.3 Augmented Reality (AR) and Virtual Reality (VR)

AR and VR are creating new opportunities for immersive and interactive marketing experiences, transforming how consumers engage with brands.

Applications in Digital Marketing:

- **Enhanced Product Visualization**: AR allows consumers to visualize products in their own space, providing a more interactive shopping experience.
    - **Example**: A furniture retailer uses an AR app to let customers see how a piece of furniture would look in their home, reducing uncertainty and increasing purchase confidence.
- **Immersive Brand Experiences**: VR offers fully immersive experiences that can transport users to virtual environments, allowing them to interact with products or explore virtual stores.
    - **Example**: A travel agency uses VR to offer virtual tours of holiday destinations, giving potential customers a taste of the experience before booking.
- **Virtual Try-Ons**: AR technology enables virtual try-ons for fashion and beauty products, allowing customers to see how items will look on them before making a purchase.
    - **Example**: A cosmetics brand uses AR to let users virtually try on different shades of lipstick, enhancing the online shopping experience.

Impact and Future Directions:

- **Increased Engagement**: AR and VR create engaging and memorable experiences, which can drive higher levels of consumer engagement and brand loyalty.
- **E-commerce Integration**: These technologies will become more integrated into e-commerce platforms, offering virtual shopping experiences and augmented product displays.
- **High Production Costs**: Developing high-quality AR and VR content requires significant investment, which may pose challenges for smaller businesses.

Sources:

- HubSpot on AR/VR in Marketing[2]
- TechCrunch on AR/VR Trends

6.2 The Future of Customer Engagement

The landscape of customer engagement is evolving, with personalization and privacy becoming central to future strategies. Understanding these dynamics is essential for building effective marketing practices.

6.2.1 Personalization

Personalization is becoming increasingly important as consumers expect tailored experiences that cater to their individual needs and preferences.

Trends in Personalization:

- **Advanced Data Use**: Leveraging customer data to create personalized marketing messages and

---

2. https://blog.hubspot.com/marketing/augmented-reality-marketing

experiences is becoming more sophisticated. Marketers use data from various touchpoints to tailor interactions.

- **Example**: E-commerce platforms use browsing history and purchase data to recommend products that are likely to interest each user, enhancing the shopping experience.

- **Dynamic Content**: Websites and email campaigns are increasingly using dynamic content that changes based on user behavior or demographics. This allows for more relevant and engaging interactions.

  - **Example**: An email marketing campaign might show different product recommendations based on a recipient's past purchases or browsing behavior.

- **Predictive Analytics**: Predictive analytics help anticipate customer needs and deliver personalized content or offers before the customer even realizes they need it.

  - **Example**: A streaming service uses predictive analytics to suggest new shows or movies based on a user's viewing habits and trends among similar users.

Impact and Future Directions:

- **Improved Customer Experiences**: Personalized marketing enhances customer satisfaction by making interactions more relevant and engaging.

- **Real-Time Adaptation**: Advances in AI will enable real-time personalization, allowing content and offers to adapt instantly to user behavior.

- **Balancing Act**: Marketers must balance personalization with respect for privacy, ensuring that data use is transparent and aligned with consumer expectations.

Sources:

- Forbes on Personalization Trends
- HubSpot on Dynamic Content[3]

6.2.2 Privacy Concerns

As digital marketing increasingly relies on data to provide personalized experiences, privacy concerns have come to the forefront. Marketers must navigate the complex landscape of data privacy to build and maintain consumer trust, comply with regulations, and avoid potential legal and reputational pitfalls.

Challenges and Solutions:

1. Data Privacy Regulations

Overview: Regulations like the General Data Protection Regulation (GDPR) in Europe and the California Consumer Privacy Act (CCPA) in the U.S. impose strict requirements on how businesses collect, store, and use personal data. These regulations aim to protect consumer privacy and give individuals greater control over their personal information.

- **GDPR**: Enacted in May 2018, GDPR requires businesses to obtain explicit consent from users before collecting their data, provide clear information on how data will be used, and allow users to access, rectify, or

---

3. https://blog.hubspot.com/marketing/dynamic-content

delete their data. Non-compliance can result in significant fines .

- Example: A website must use a cookie consent banner that clearly explains what data is being collected and for what purpose, and must obtain user consent before placing cookies on their device.

- **CCPA**: Effective since January 2020, CCPA gives California residents the right to know what personal information is being collected, the ability to opt out of the sale of their data, and the right to request deletion of their data .

  - Example: An online retailer must provide a "Do Not Sell My Personal Information" link on their website, allowing users to opt out of data sales.

Impact: Compliance with these regulations requires businesses to implement robust data management practices and ensure transparency in their data collection and usage processes. Failure to comply can lead to substantial financial penalties and damage to reputation.

2. Transparency and Consent

Overview: Being transparent about data collection practices and obtaining explicit consent from users helps build trust and ensures compliance with legal requirements. Transparency involves clearly communicating what data is collected, how it will be used, and providing users with control over their information.

- **Consent Mechanisms**: Implement clear consent mechanisms, such as cookie banners and opt-in forms, that allow users to make informed decisions about their data.

- ◦ **Example**: An e-commerce site might use a pop-up that explains its data collection practices and asks users to consent to cookies that track browsing behavior for personalized recommendations.

- **Privacy Policies**: Develop comprehensive privacy policies that are easy to understand and readily accessible. These policies should outline data collection practices, the purpose of data use, and users' rights regarding their data .

  - ◦ **Example**: A company's privacy policy should detail how user data is collected, stored, and used, and provide contact information for privacy-related inquiries.

Impact: Transparency and consent build consumer trust, making users more likely to share their data willingly. Clear communication and easy-to-use consent options also improve user experience and reduce friction.

3. Data Security

Overview: Protecting personal data from breaches and unauthorized access is crucial for maintaining consumer trust and complying with data privacy regulations. Data security involves implementing technical measures and best practices to safeguard personal information.

- **Encryption**: Use encryption to protect sensitive data both in transit and at rest. Encryption helps ensure that data is unreadable to unauthorized parties .

- ○ **Example**: An online payment system should use SSL/
  TLS encryption to secure transactions and protect
  credit card information.
- **Access Controls**: Implement strict access controls to
  limit who can access personal data. Use authentication
  mechanisms and role-based access controls to ensure
  that only authorized personnel can view or handle
  sensitive information .
  - ○ **Example**: A CRM system should restrict access to
    customer data based on employee roles, ensuring that
    only those who need to know can view or edit
    information.
- **Regular Security Audits**: Conduct regular security
  audits and vulnerability assessments to identify and
  address potential weaknesses in data protection
  measures .
  - ○ **Example**: A company might perform quarterly security
    audits to evaluate its data protection practices and
    ensure compliance with industry standards.

Impact: Strong data security measures help prevent data breaches and unauthorized access, protecting both the business and its customers. Demonstrating a commitment to data security can enhance brand reputation and customer loyalty.

4. Ethical Data Use

Overview: Beyond legal compliance, ethical considerations in data use involve respecting user privacy and using data in ways that align with consumer expectations and values. Ethical data use fosters trust and supports sustainable business practices.

- **Minimal Data Collection**: Collect only the data necessary for the intended purpose, avoiding excessive or intrusive data collection .
  - Example: An online survey should ask only for information relevant to the survey's objectives, rather than collecting extensive personal details.
- **Data Anonymization**: Use data anonymization techniques to protect individual privacy while still gaining insights from aggregated data .
  - Example: A health app might anonymize user data when analyzing trends to ensure individual users' health information remains private.
- **User Empowerment**: Empower users to control their data through easy-to-use privacy settings and clear options for managing their information .
  - Example: Social media platforms should provide clear settings that allow users to control who can see their posts and what personal information is shared.

Impact: Ethical data practices enhance consumer trust and loyalty by aligning business operations with user expectations and societal values. Companies that prioritize ethical data use are better positioned to build long-term relationships with their customers.

Conclusion of Chapter 6

Chapter 6 explored the cutting-edge technologies and emerging trends shaping the future of digital marketing and customer engagement.

MODERN DIGITAL MARKETING STRATEGIES FOR A CONNECTED WORLD

Emerging Technologies: AI, Voice Search, and AR/VR are revolutionizing digital marketing by enabling more personalized, interactive, and efficient marketing practices. AI offers powerful tools for data analysis and personalization, Voice Search changes the SEO landscape by emphasizing natural language queries, and AR/VR provide immersive experiences that enhance consumer engagement.

Future of Customer Engagement: The future of customer engagement hinges on balancing personalization with privacy concerns. While advances in technology enable deeper personalization, they also raise significant privacy issues. Navigating data privacy regulations, maintaining transparency, and implementing robust data security measures are crucial for building and maintaining consumer trust.

Chapter 7: Conclusion and Next Steps

In this final chapter, we summarize the key takeaways from our exploration of digital marketing, provide additional resources for further learning, and outline actionable steps for readers to implement the insights gained throughout this eBook.

7.1 Summary of Key Takeaways

1. Fundamentals of Digital Marketing

- **Definition and Scope**: Digital marketing involves leveraging online channels to promote products and services, offering broader reach, cost-effectiveness, and real-time engagement compared to traditional marketing.
- **Core Components**: Key components include Search Engine Optimization (SEO), content marketing, social media marketing, and email marketing. Each plays a crucial role in driving traffic, engaging audiences, and generating leads .

2. Strategies and Techniques

- **SEO**: Effective SEO enhances your website's visibility on search engines through keyword optimization, quality content, and technical improvements .
- **Content Marketing**: Creating valuable and engaging content helps attract and retain audiences. A well-planned content strategy involves understanding your

audience, developing a content calendar, and measuring performance .

- **Social Media Marketing**: Leveraging social media platforms to connect with your audience, build brand awareness, and drive traffic involves choosing the right platforms, creating engaging content, and monitoring performance .
- **Email Marketing**: Building and managing an email list, crafting effective emails, and personalizing content are key to successful email marketing campaigns .

3. Tools and Resources

- **Analytics**: Tools like Google Analytics and social media analytics provide insights into your performance, helping to refine strategies and improve outcomes .
- **Automation**: Email automation and social media scheduling tools streamline marketing efforts, improving efficiency and consistency .
- **SEO Tools**: Keyword research and on-page optimization tools aid in enhancing search engine rankings .
- **Content Management Systems**: Platforms like WordPress and HubSpot CMS facilitate content creation and management .
- **Design and Multimedia**: Tools for graphic design and video editing help create engaging visuals and multimedia content .

4. Trends and Future Directions

- **Emerging Technologies**: AI, voice search, and AR/VR are transforming digital marketing by enabling more personalized, interactive, and efficient strategies .
- **Future of Customer Engagement**: Personalization is becoming increasingly important, while privacy concerns require careful management of data collection and usage .

7.2 Additional Resources and Reading

To deepen your understanding of digital marketing and stay updated with the latest trends, consider exploring the following resources:

- **Books**:
    - *"Digital Marketing for Dummies"* by Ryan Deiss and Russ Henneberry: A comprehensive guide covering all aspects of digital marketing.
    - *"Content Inc."* by Joe Pulizzi: Focuses on building a content-first business model.
- **Websites**:
    - HubSpot Blog[1]: Offers articles and guides on various digital marketing topics.
    - Moz: Provides insights and resources on SEO and digital marketing trends.
- **Courses**:
    - Google Digital Garage: Free online courses covering a wide range of digital marketing

---

1. https://blog.hubspot.com/

topics.

- Coursera Digital Marketing Specialization[2]: A series of courses covering fundamental and advanced digital marketing skills.

- **Podcasts**:
  - *"Marketing School"* with Neil Patel and Eric Siu: Daily episodes offering digital marketing tips and strategies.
  - *"Online Marketing Made Easy"* with Amy Porterfield: Provides insights and strategies for successful digital marketing campaigns.

- **Research and Reports**:
  - eMarketer[3]: Provides data and insights on digital marketing trends and forecasts.
  - Statista[4]: Offers statistics and studies on various aspects of digital marketing.

7.3 Actionable Next Steps for Readers

Based on the knowledge gained throughout this eBook, here are actionable steps to help you implement effective digital marketing strategies:

1. Define Clear Goals

- **Set SMART Objectives**: Determine specific, measurable, achievable, relevant, and time-bound goals that align with your business objectives.
  - **Example**: If your goal is to increase website traffic, set a target such as "Increase website traffic by 20% over the

---

2. https://www.coursera.org/specializations/digital-marketing

3. https://www.emarketer.com/

4. https://www.statista.com/

next quarter through a combination of SEO and content marketing."

2. Develop a Comprehensive Plan

- **Create a Digital Marketing Plan**: Outline your strategies for SEO, content marketing, social media, and email marketing. Include a budget and a timeline for each activity.
  - ○ **Example**: Develop a content calendar that includes weekly blog posts, daily social media updates, and monthly email newsletters.

3. Leverage the Right Tools

- **Use Analytics and Automation Tools**: Implement tools like Google Analytics for tracking performance and Hootsuite for automating social media posts.
  - ○ **Example**: Use Google Analytics to monitor traffic sources and identify which channels are driving the most visitors to your site.

4. Optimize for Emerging Technologies

- **Adapt to New Trends**: Stay updated with the latest trends in AI, voice search, and AR/VR. Experiment with these technologies to enhance your marketing efforts.
  - ○ **Example**: Optimize your website content for voice search by including natural language queries and FAQs.

5. Focus on Personalization and Privacy

- **Implement Personalization**: Use data insights to

tailor your marketing messages and offers to individual
user preferences.

- ◦ **Example**: Personalize email campaigns based on user
  behavior, such as previous purchases or browsing
  history.
- **Ensure Data Privacy Compliance**: Stay compliant
  with data privacy regulations like GDPR and CCPA.
  Be transparent about your data collection practices and
  obtain user consent.
  - ◦ **Example**: Update your privacy policy and provide clear
    options for users to manage their data preferences.

6. Monitor and Adjust Your Strategy

- **Track Performance**: Regularly monitor the
  performance of your campaigns using KPIs and
  metrics.
  - ◦ **Example**: Analyze engagement metrics for your social
    media posts and adjust your content strategy based on
    what resonates most with your audience.
- **Make Data-Driven Decisions**: Use the insights
  gained from analytics to refine and improve your
  marketing strategies.
  - ◦ **Example**: If a particular ad campaign is
    underperforming, experiment with different ad
    creatives or targeting options to optimize results.

By following these steps, you can effectively implement the
digital marketing strategies discussed in this eBook, adapt to
emerging trends, and build a strong foundation for ongoing

success in the digital landscape. Stay informed, be adaptable, and continuously refine your approach based on data and feedback to achieve your marketing objectives.

Final Words to the Reader

As we conclude this eBook on digital marketing, I want to extend my heartfelt thanks for joining me on this journey. The landscape of digital marketing is both dynamic and vast, constantly evolving with new technologies and trends. The chapters you've explored here are designed to provide you with a solid foundation and actionable insights to help you navigate and thrive in this ever-changing field.

Reflecting on Your Journey

Throughout these pages, we've delved into the essential components of digital marketing, from understanding the fundamentals to implementing advanced strategies. Each chapter aimed to equip you with the knowledge and tools needed to enhance your marketing efforts, connect more effectively with your audience, and achieve your business objectives.

- **Understanding the Basics**: You started with a deep dive into the fundamentals of digital marketing, gaining a comprehensive view of how different strategies and techniques come together to create a cohesive approach.
- **Developing Strategies**: You learned about the critical importance of SEO, content marketing, social media, and email marketing, understanding how each element plays a role in driving traffic, engaging audiences, and generating leads.
- **Leveraging Tools and Technologies**: You explored various tools and technologies that can streamline your

efforts and provide valuable insights, helping you to implement and optimize your marketing strategies more effectively.

- **Adapting to Trends**: You gained insights into emerging trends and future directions, preparing you to stay ahead of the curve and adapt to the changing landscape of digital marketing.

Your Path Forward

As you take the next steps in your digital marketing journey, remember that the key to success lies in continuous learning and adaptation. The world of digital marketing is fast-paced and ever-evolving, but with the right mindset and strategies, you can turn challenges into opportunities.

- **Stay Curious**: Always seek out new knowledge, whether through additional reading, courses, or industry events. Staying informed about the latest trends and technologies will keep your skills sharp and your strategies effective.
- **Be Adaptable**: Flexibility is crucial in digital marketing. Be prepared to adjust your strategies based on performance data, emerging trends, and changes in consumer behavior.
- **Focus on Your Audience**: At the heart of every successful marketing campaign is a deep understanding of your audience. Continue to listen, engage, and adapt to their needs and preferences.

Final Thoughts

MODERN DIGITAL MARKETING STRATEGIES FOR A CONNECTED WORLD

The journey to mastering digital marketing is ongoing, filled with opportunities to learn, grow, and innovate. As you apply the insights and strategies from this eBook, I encourage you to approach each challenge with creativity and resilience. Your commitment to understanding and leveraging the power of digital marketing will not only enhance your business but also foster meaningful connections with your audience.

Thank you for embarking on this journey with me. I wish you all the best in your digital marketing endeavors. May your strategies be innovative, your campaigns successful, and your engagement with your audience rewarding and impactful.

Happy marketing!